WORK,
WHERE DREAMS GO TO DIE

A SARCASTIC COLORING BOOK TO MAKE YOU LAUGH AFTER A LONG DAY AT THE OFFICE

Do you ever come home from work asking yourself what you are doing with your life? Questioning every life choice because your job is slowly sucking the soul out of you. Give yourself a few minutes to relax and laugh with this easy, sarcastic, and sometimes inappropriate adult coloring book. Filled with the things you want to say out loud at the office but don't because you need a paycheck. 27 fun pages sprinkled with sayings you would only share with your favorite funny coworkers.

Happy coloring!

THE NINJA

The full of shit asshole who weasels their way out of work.

HAVE YOU SEEN MY

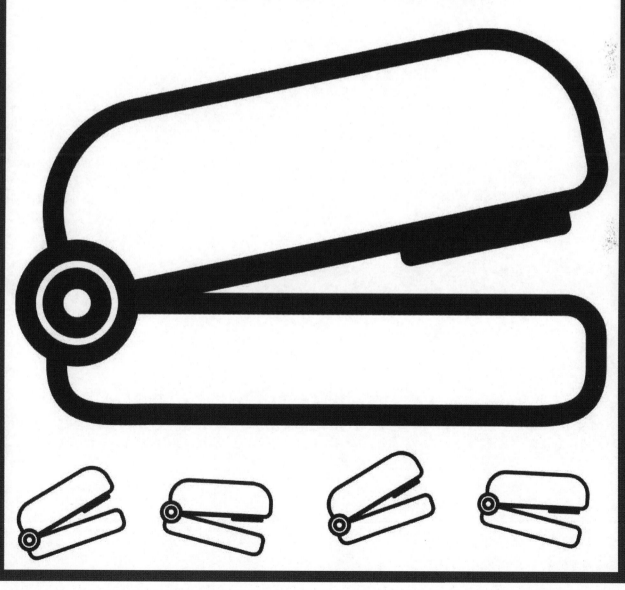

My face when the LAZIEST coworker complains about working hard.

Thank you so much for heating
your smelly FISH
on your lunch break.

When you pull up to work and the building is still standing.

When people ask how I
handle my job....

pretty sure
I'M DEAD INSIDE

AS PER MY
MY
PREVIOUS EMAIL

OFFICE TRIBE

The sarcastic group of bitches who make your job less miserable.

When someone asks you a dumb question at work.

The brilliant asshole who can do no wrong in the eyes of management.

THE ALL STAR

How come you never stress out at work? What's your secret?

CHOOSE WISELY

REPLY

REPLY ALL

When you forgot to hit the
mute button

and everyone's looking at you.

I'd tell you to go to

HELL

but I

there and
I don't
want
to see you

WORK

EVERYDAY

Not my circus, not my monkeys. But I can definitely point out the

CLOWNS

because

WORK

My boss says I intimidate my coworkers, so I stared at him until he apologized.

When someone marks
every email

URGENT

How to be a mature grown-up at work:

replace

"FUCK YOU"

with

"OK, GREAT"

What bonuses should look like:

reality...

$10 GAS CARD

The greatest thing to happen to every customer service employee with a

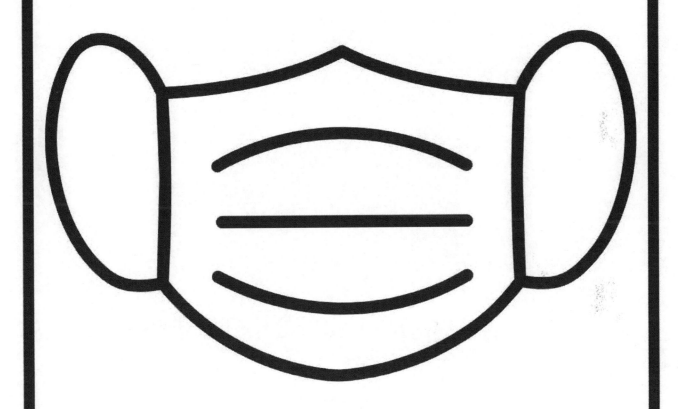

RESTING BITCH FACE

From the author

Thank you so much for buying and coloring this book. I sincerely hope it cheered you up and made you laugh out loud.

Would you please take a few more minutes to leave me a review? Every review helps and I would truly appreciate it!

 Thank you!

Made in the USA
Columbia, SC
27 December 2022

74996885R00033